Praises for Juaquina She

"This book was inspiring. It was everything you could expect of a book of poems. I appreciate Juaquina and her bravery in diving so deep and reminding me that in the darkest moments are where you find your light." - Kiara Surun, Author of *'Versed'*

"JuaquinaShe isn't just a writer, although she does that pretty dang well. JuaquinaShe lives the love she writes about. Her words are a soft place to just be. Her words reek of lived experience. They reek of intimacy and holiness. JuaquinaShe is an alchemist and a wordsmith. Her words remind you that being human is a dangerously beautiful thing. You'll be glad you read her." -Kariah Rose, Poet

"Okay, no joke, just reading your bio made me cry. Feels like a landing, like a safe place to sit and be honest. Wow, thanks for existing" -Taylor W.

Dedication

This is for the person God is speaking to. The one
questioning everything. The one struggling to find
meaning in an ever changing world. The one reaching for
their dreams but not sure where to start. The ones who
desperately want to move forward. Let this book serve as
a tool to lay the foundation.

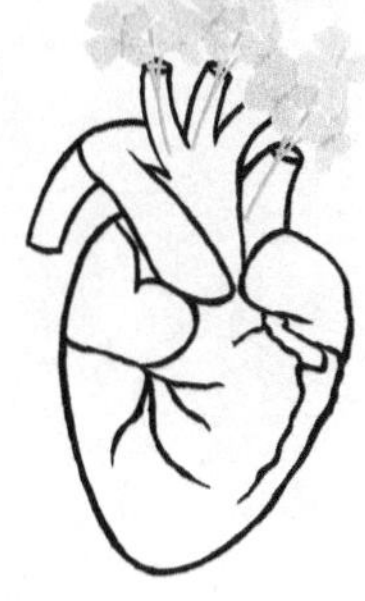

Royalty

juaqnina she

Sections

juaquina she

WHO

Not a rhetorical question

Who are you?

God:
I want you to see just how much bondage you're in.
Look at it. Become aware of the gravity of it all.
It's a truth you don't like.
I got you, okay?
Do you trust me?

Me: I do.

A Fool's Paradise

I've learned
When I pray
The devil is listening also
And he seems to answer quicker than God most times
But he offers *lies*

He gives me lust
And calls it love

...and I seem to fall for that shit every fucking time.

They told me:

I wasn't good enough.

Loss after love

Damn
I don't want to write all about heartbreak
But I never seem as motivated
Until I'm reminded how it feels
To be alone
After
Being loved

You tell me it's over through a text message
That's some fucked up shit.

This pain in my chest
Was caused by a man who has probably already forgotten me
They tell me not to question my worth when someone leaves
But how can I not?
I just want to know what I did wrong...

But it's probably best that he didn't give me an explanation
Because I would have spent years trying to contort myself into
his box

I would have walked further away from who I really am

But still...
I wonder why he left

juaquina She

Memories of You

His scent lingers on your side of the bed
My attempt to rid me of your memories
Has only left me irritated
Has only left me planning a trip to the laundromat
I try to replace you
But his hands aren't large enough
His conversation isn't good enough
To distract me
From your absence
From this consistent feeling that I made a mistake
From the trembling in my feet as I convince myself not to run back
Not to settle
Because a part of me believes
Loving a piece of you is better than having none of you

Restricted Grief

I miss you
No I mean...

                                        ...I...

                                                        ...miss you.

No other words can form
Because no other words make sense
No other words describe the blood that drips slow
From my heart onto the ground
But I can't
I'm not allowed to say
What I really feel
Because we have no relationship
We are not and were not ever together
You were not mine

                        ...but I was yours

I was your pillow to lay on
I was your soft hands to hold
I was your keeper of secrets
No other number would your fingers dial when you were upset
I was your everything
So you should miss me
Why don't you miss me?!
The day it ended
You got up and walked away
But your shadow stayed
It haunts me
The silhouette of you reminds me of broken dreams
Lost hopes
That shattered
The moment you decided
The relationship we didn't have
Had ran its course

                                        But what about me?

juaquina She

Lost in a relationship

I lost my shadow
Searching for the light in your darkness
I drowned in you and couldn't find a way out
Your energy was one to consume
Leaving little room for the sun to remind the earth that I'm here

They told me:

I wasn't pretty enough

Shame on the men who invite us into a love they never
planned to show up for

I didn't realize I was slipping
Into your darkness
I was wearing your scars
As if they were my own
When our bodies connected
So did our souls
And I rose with more baggage
Than what I laid down with
But I loved you enough
To not let that stop me

Sex; A Power Struggle

Well before you read my poetry
You assigned my body value
So I use it as my weapon
When I feel my weakest
I bend my body the way you like it
I need your companionship
But you only offer your attention

So I take it

So I hold all the power

You cannot comfort me
When I have gone numb inside

My Vice, My Friend

Being sober
Is overrated
The damage done
By my vices
Almost seem worth it
When staring in the face of the demons
I wish to escape
But running to what kills me
Doesn't kill my demons
It only locks myself in a closet
So that I can hide
And pretend
If only for a moment
That this monster doesn't exist

I will admit

I allow the wrong people to camp out on in my heart

I confess

I don't even know who the right people are

They told me:

I was selfish

Life can be a Bitter Cup to Drink From

How do I embrace
Everything God brings me
When it does not match my prayers?

How do I form thank you
On my lips
When my circumstances make me bitter?

How do I worship
In despair?

juaqnina She

They told me:

I shouldn't talk so loudly.

I have decided to just lie
When people ask me how I am

People only like to talk to me about my depression in past tense as if my reality is to heavy but somehow my testimony is easy to carry. Do they want me to be over it? They want me to say I *used* to cry. I *used* to lose sleep. I *used* to be manic then crash. But what if the cycle never stopped? What if my skies are grey <u>right now</u>? What if it is taking all of my willpower to smile <u>right now</u>?

Anxious Thoughts

Nothing inside of me has been resting
My spirit twitches with angst
My soul paces the floor in worry
My mind flies through vices
My hands reach for something...anything
Besides this.
I want to be anywhere but here
The problem is
I have been trying to escape for so long
I don't even remember what I'm running from

What is it that troubles me?

I'm sorry for Being Depressed

Sometimes
I cry
And I find myself apologizing

To who?
                    God.
                Myself.
            The world.

Apologizing for my existence
That it's so complicated
That my emotions take up so much space
That they come in without explanation
Tear up everything
Then settle again

Returning to Self (part two)

I only give people a mild version of myself
I only tell them about pieces of my depression
I only offer a toned down dose of my happiness
I don't express my silliness and how I often take a joke too far
I put myself on a leash around others
And that is why it is so hard to remember myself
When I'm home alone
Dealing with a shadow of who I really am

Do you ever feel guilty just for existing?

All the time.

I can't hear the music anymore.

They told me...

I know what "they" say

...But who are "they" that tell me this? Perhaps my own insecurities. Perhaps the evil spirit that lurks in this world. "They" are not attached to singular people. They are a force that doesn't wish for me to know who I truly am, because I am made in the image of God himself. I am a walking divine entity, and I could partner with God to create the Garden of Eden.

What does God say?

God: Do you feel like you missed something?

Me: Yes.

God: You cannot miss the kingdom of God.

ARE

Perspective

Why does the cage seem so enticing to a free man?
Why does the path of liberation feel so foreign to his feet?

Whom the son sets free is truly free indeed
But what do I do now?
I often longed for this moment but I guess I never thought
about what happens next
The door swings open
The light breaks the silence
The noose around my neck is severed
And now...I am free

It takes me a moment though...
To register what happened.
Then a sudden joy embraces me as the tears of excitement
wash me clean
I jump, I shout, I talk about it
I'm happy.
But I haven't stepped out of the prison yet
I just stand in amazement that I now have the ability to leave
So I start to tell people about it, I scream from inside the cage
that I am free!
"Look at me! My future is open, and the possibilities are
endless.
God has come, and He has kept His promises!"

Perspective Cont.

But I don't step foot out of what has now become a
torturous zone of comfort
Because....what is outside of the cage?
I dreamed it would contain a world beyond anything I
have ever seen
Where I could hold my head high
Where I could defeat the enemies attacks
Where the weapons would not prosper
Where my nightmares didn't keep my awake at night
Where the demons no longer called me by name
Where my light could shine
Where I could be everything God said I was....a girl I
never met before
And now as I stare at the mirror and see a stranger
gazing back...
I am afraid.
This woman looks.....jubilant, fearless, at peace with who
she is and where she is going
But I do not know her
I remember the girl with fear in her eyes as the darkness
slowly emptied her lungs
Until she could no longer take a breath without killing a
part of herself
She was ugly
But she was familiar
I knew her
I was her
And I was comfortable

Perspective Cont.

always dreamed of wearing a crown
But now it seems too heavy to remain on my head
The jewels scratch my scalp
The the glare of the sun hitting the gold blinds anyone that
looks my way
So I don't have a lot of friends
People seem to love the thought of me but lack the
enthusiasm to actually talk to me

I'm not sure I like this
I mean...I love this!
Please don't take it away
I just....I don't know what to do with it
It's something I have never experienced before

Mostly everyone I've known my entire life
Are watching me peer out from the open door of my cage
With curiosity in their eyes
And I can't help but to feel guilty....as they have to watch me
behind bars that hold them captive
The people I love are suffering....maybe I should pretend we
are still the same
Maybe......no I must leave
Before the door closes again
Before the darkness drowns me
The light coming in isn't as bright as it was before
I can't lose a moment to step into a world I've only faith-ed
were real
No sight, just hopes

Perspective Cont.

Whom the son sets free is truly free indeed
But why does my eyes wander back to the cage?
Why do I find my gaze drifting back to my confinement
while standing in green pastures
The water is still
But my habits are convulsing
I don't have to do it
But it feels weird not to behave as if I still have chains around
my wrists
It feels strange to roam freely and no longer be bound by
shackles
I always believed we were meant to be limitless
But....I must confess

I'm scared.

The journey to freedom is scary
The path of healing can be lonely
Sometimes the comfort zone built in the brokenness
Tempts me to run back
But I must continue forward

In the beginning
There was chaos
And God's spirit
hovered
Over the chaos

In the beginning
There was chaos
A dark void of
Nothing
And God's spirit
Hovered

Over the chaotic nothingness

In the beginning
There was God
There was chaos
And there was an opportunity for God to respond

And He did.

In the beginning there was God
There was a chaotic mass of nothing
And God's response was
To create.

"Let there be light."

So, in the beginning
Of a new chapter in my life
When presented with
Nothing and Chaos

I will create.

Stream of Consciousness (Panic Attack)

I feel lost in the world.

I'm not sure how to feel. It feels like a storm brewing
inside of me and I don't event know how to begin to
understand it.

What's at the heart of this storm?
Fear.

How can I speak to my storm and tell it to be still. Use
the power Jesus had. Which was? The Holy Spirit.
Okay...lol how do I use that power? By believing.

Everywhere I go I'm carrying the weight of my bills. Of
my grief. Of my shame around my sexuality. Of my
trauma. Of my diagnosis. It's hard to talk about because
I'm very sensitive and I don't want to let anyone in on
something I haven't unpacked for myself yet. But I
shouldn't be doing this alone. Period.

My energy is calm but focused. Steady but always
working. My energy is powerful. My energy is a force.

I cannot panic. Breathe.

Breathe.
Breathe.
Breathe.
One breath turns into two
Just breathe.

God: It's going to take time for you to feel alright and that's alright.

Every night I break down
And
God builds me back up

I thought you had died
In my daydreams
I don't create those anymore
I thought when I gave up fantasy
I gave up you
I thought your voice had been muted
By the bruises on my heart
I thought
Maybe...you didn't exist anymore
At least not for me
When I close my eyes
Nightmares fill my sleep
I thought maybe you forgot about me
In the midst of all this chaos
I thought your hands were too full
To massage me back to peace.

Who am I talking to?

Answer:hope

I sit alone with my thoughts
And they terrify me
But I am learning
Not to run away from my own vastness
The universe inside of me
Cannot destroy me
The masters tools cannot dismantle the masters house
So I, as tool, cannot destroy the plan God has for me
And I, as master, cannot be destroyed by my own emotions

juaqmina She

Have you ever met a guy
Who is in love with your light
Until he thinks it too bright
Until he is challenged in his views
Until his truth is exposed
And the truth is
He hates feminism.

I have to unlearn everything
That loving you taught me

juaquina She

Imitation

I would rather spend my nights alone
Feel the emptiness of no one on the other side of my bed
Than to accept your broken shards of love
I would rather die from loneliness
Than to bleed from false love

Stab me in my heart than ask me what's wrong
Paint me with the color green
Then call me crazy
As if I chose this

You walked into my life
Confidently
As if you were going to offer something real knowing damn well
you didn't even want me
I am a human
With a real heart
Not something to pass the time
Don't fetishize the artist in me
The dancer in me
The flexible parts of me
The passion within me
Don't pervert what's supposed to be beautiful
What's supposed to be potent
Don't extract the sexuality
Then refuse the covenant

Imitation (cont.)

I am not a fantasy
I am real
My pain is real
My love is real
How I feel about you is real
The room that I created in my heart for you is real

You are not obligated to reciprocate
But don't you dare imitate
Just to get what you want
Don't you dare offer me half of what I deserve
Don't you dare treat me like I'm asking for too much
Don't you dare tease me with something you will never give me

Their complements
Won't erase your rejection

juaquina She

The Moment I Realized
You Would Never Step Up To The Plate

I saw it in your eyes
I remember the day
I remember the moment
The flash of realization when you knew you should be
treating me better
For just a second
I saw a longing, a softness in your eyes
For me
A channel to your heart sent out a signal
And I noticed

But

Your actions did not change.

So I left.

Question:
Why are you trying to be good enough for a man who is not
good enough for you?

Walk away.

The Meeting.

When I decided to leave you behind
I had an internal meeting
My heart, my womb, my vagina, and my soul all had
a say so
And even though you touched all parts of me
We were all ready to let you go
Except my heart...
She had a few conditions
To which I will not list
But if you were to do these things she made me
agree to give you a second chance
To which I complied

And now I hope you will force me to forgive you
But only sincerity can do that
And sometimes I question if you're capable of that.

The Reason I Have to Burn That Bridge

I cannot love somebody who feels like a prison.

There are moments
When I feel like myself again
Small glimpses back into a girl who was unafraid of life
But that girl was flawed wasn't she?
She led me here
Down this rabbit hole
I guess I shouldn't romanticize the girl before the trauma
Because she had no idea how to adjust
How to cope
When the rug is snatched from under her
Which is fair
But not practical
So while I want my joy
And my courageous spirit to return
I do not wish for the girl who becomes paralyzed
When the plot takes a twists
Because life must keep going, right?
So now, I reach my hands forward
And I study

Lord, how do I learn to keep moving when my heart has
been snatched from me?

juaquina She

God: You rest the first time I tell you to. You don't wait six months. You don't wait for your anxiety to become unbearable. You take note of the first time you must call out of work because of your mental health. You step out of survival mode, and you heal. Leaning into our partnership. Knowing that I would never allow your healing to interfere with your purpose. You will reach everything I want you to, everything you were created to. But you must first take care of you. What good is a train that breaks down between stops? Learn regular maintenance of you.

Shabbat

I no   longer want to be at war with myself
Anxiety feels like being stuck in flight and fight
And I'm tired
My soul cannot hold this stance for much longer
She must rest
All the women in me are tired
The one who carries the bipolar
The one who wears the anxiety
The one who is parenting my inner child
The one who is planning a future as a writer
We
She is tired
A type of exhaustion sleep will never cure
But maybe these words will
Maybe allowing it to all spill over on this page
Will cause the inner tsunami to subside
The earthquakes to settle
And stop disrupting my daily routine
Maybe the only way to win this battle
Is to stop fighting
And simply rest
On a spiritual level
Maybe
It's time to
Shabbat

I'm sorry for the things I said
I was speaking from my wound.

juaquina She

unforgiveness starts to feel like a weapon when it's really a cage.

Dear self, where did I leave you last?

Searching for answers
In every fortune cookie
Every wishing well
I hope to find a sign that leads me to you
Through every butterfly that crosses my path
Every rainbow after a rainstorm
I almost hear God whispering
Affirmations that my love is not in vain

Message From My Heart

Don't love that man
Don't believe them when they make it seem like
isolation is normal
You need friends who will try to help even when they
don't understand your pain
Go to counseling. At least try it.
You need to quit that job
You need to be honest with your mom
You need to walk away from this toxic behavior
You will heal with your dad but don't force it before it's
time.
Be diligent but patient with yourself
I don't like it when you allow guys to love parts of you
without a commitment.
I'm lonely but I still have standards and I still believe you
deserve the love you want.
I believe it exists and I believe God is bringing it to your
life.
I believe all of your preparation is not in vain
I believe you will do what you want
And what you think
And what you have always known you would
Just be you.
No on is you and that is your power.

I want you to know these words will still have meaning
even when you're not crying and when you feel sober
minded. These are still your truths. My truths. I love you.
You will get better but the sober you, the sober me has
to put in the work that the hurt me desperately needs.

God: listen my daughter and hear my words very clearly. I want to talk to you. I want you to know how special you are to me. You mean the world to me. I love you, daughter. I care for you

God: Man will never set you free. It's me. I am the only one with that power. No job, no human, no career, no passion has the ability to release you from any source of bondage. Only I can do that. And when I do, it is immediate. You only have to learn how to walk in your freedom.

Me: Lord, teach me to walk in my freedom from you through Christ.

God: I will

Grieving means finding a way to make peace with what
has gone because search how you may, you will never
be able to replace a love that is no more (because love
experiences are like snowflakes) so you must find a way
to enter into gracious acceptance. And that shit is hard.
This is why grief is a process and takes time.

Sometimes I am able to accept your new residence
Sometimes I wake up
With the spirit of all those I grieve sleeping in my bed

Acceptance is not the last step in grief.
It's the first step in healing.
And my dear you will have to hold hands with your grief as
you heal.

The Mother Pt. 1

To the guys I loved in seasons passed.
I was so afraid of painting you as villains
Because I know the hero inside of you
I know the human
The story that made the man
I know your heart was not created for evil
But I can no longer ignore my own pain to nurture your ego
I pretend that what you did wasn't as damaging as it was
But why do I find myself mothering my aggressor
What a learned behavior of a survivor of trauma
Nursing the wounds of the ones that hurt me
Trying to spare their guilt
While allowing my wounds to become untreated and infected

A Word from God
I love you.

What type of love are you looking for?

 Radical acceptance
Loyal freedom &
Unending intimacy

I have to stop compromising what I want.

Let go
Stop tap dancing for everyone around you
Stop entertaining them to keep their attention
And see who stays
See who believes your existence is enough
Grieve the ones who leave
Then celebrate whoever is left
They are your chosen family

Last night I had a dream that I had a miscarriage

God: I need you to listen to me and breathe. I am here. I am what you need to get by. I am your source and I love you.

Me: I don't want to abort my dreams.

God: You won't. Leave them to me. You have not yet walked away, and I want you to stay here with me. I know you are hurting. You think no one understands but I am right here with you. I know about the rejection and the hurt feelings.

Me: God I'm so confused about everything. Everyone including myself seems to think I have given up, but I have not. I just needed to look away for a second. I just needed to get my bearings together. Life has been happening and I just need a second to stand on solid ground for a while before I keep walking, and I don't think that's a bad thing.

God: It's not. Trust me. Allow me to lead you. What is inside of you will never leave. That's how you internalized what happened (the dream), but that is not what happened. You only lose what you walk away from. Trust me. I am inside of you. I am around you. I am here. Do not allow others to force their thinking or lifestyles on you. Rid yourself of opinions. Rid yourself of that junk. If it does not resonate with your soul, let it go. Don't allow it to affect you. You are my child. Not theirs. Mine. You belong to me and I to you. Let us be one and continue on this journey ahead.

Oceans

Here I stand on the shore of forever
And stare at my doubts
They are called the ocean
A mass of mystery
A current of strength
That want to pull me under
I panic
I think I'm sinking
Until I look down
And see my feet have not left the shore
It is true
I am still safe
But where have I gone?
No where.

Dancing around the flames
That threaten to consume us
This is how we cast spells
Onto the darkness
That overshadows and tries to threaten our joy
In the presence of despair
We dance

The call us witches
But we are just trying to heal

juaquina she

I must be brave.

My fears don't hit the same
I guess when you are forced
To face the things you once ran from
Perspective slows down fight or flight
Now I process and respond
The pain still hits hard
But I am learning to get through I must strive for acceptance
Submission
To Gods will

God: I look out for you. Your mental health and physical health comes first. Everything else is secondary. Who you are and how you are as a person is my first concern. You are my beloved daughter. I cherish you so. I love you.

I will love again
I will be loved by a man
He will look at me with stars in his eyes
He will be mature enough and emotionally intelligent
enough to recognize and understand that I am worth
sacrifice. I am worth pursuit.
I deserve good things.
I deserve to be happy.
I deserve to smile.
I will love again.
And he will love me.
He will respect me and my feelings
He will love me
He will call me beautiful and believe it
He will not tear me down
He will be great
The love we share will be great
We will be great
We will be a reflection of Gods love to everyone
I will love again
I will be loved
I will be pursued
I will be loved and pursued.

Not only will I be loved by one man
I will receive love from creation
Everything around me will be in harmony
With God's plan for my life
I will heal
I will love myself
I will experience community
I will experience healthy family bonds
I will love
And I will be loved
By what and who God has for me
This is not acceptance for all mankind
But from who I am destined to share a tribe with

Yes, not only will I love

I will be loved.

YOU?

A Word from God

It's time to let go of the past
It's time to enter into a new thing
Walk on a new path

Vision: I am kneeling on a path made of Gold. God walks towards me. My head is bowed. He is dressed like a king. He touches my chin to lift my head. When I look up I see light. I feel something coming up from my throat. I open my mouth and the words I love you come out. Then the words seem to create beautiful vegetation all around. Green grass and a prosperous land. I stand. and walk out towards what I see. It is good.

God: all you have to do is love me.

Me: Show me how.

God: I will

I have to let you go now
I have to love myself now
I have to hold hands with God
And run towards the sun now
Because I've spent too many nights staring at the moon
And darkness is not my home
I have to live in the light now
I have to walk in self discovery now
I have to be loved now
Because you weren't offering me that
Just compromise

I fell in love with a guy
Who was in love with mediocrity
I tried to contort myself
To fit what he likes
But my calling doesn't fit into a box
Ironic
Trying to grow to be good enough for him
Is what pushed him away
Because of his love for average

Growth

When sifting through old thoughts
Like photographs in the attic
I come across a few snapshots of you
A week ago I would have held them in my hands
And stared until the pictures seemed to move again
Until memory morphed into future
Today I know I cannot change a picture into a movie
I cannot twist what was into something that could never be
Today, I cannot and will not linger too long
A glance is enough to confirm you are not what I want

Before, I asked myself if I was good enough
Now, I don't bother with foolish questions
It is not about worth
It is about what belongs to me
And being around you made me question what was
promised
Made me compromise on the peace of mind I had without
you
I based my worth on your actions
And you turned away from me every time
So I learned to hate myself with my habits
I learned to beg for validation
That was a week ago

Today I look at myself
And realize you were never meant to be mine
Who you are and who I am simply do not fit
Today I realized, you're not even my type
I held the thought
I looked upon the memory and considered throwing it away
I will keep it as a reminder
To never again search for an answer
Only found within

Affirmation:

I am beautiful.

I won't listen to them anymore
The men who tell me I am not enough
I will not look through their eyes
When I see myself
When they tell me I am not pretty enough
I will not use their ears to listen to my own words
My own thoughts
When they tell me what I have to say is not important
I will not use their perspective
When viewing my world
Because
Truth be told
I love me

It Was Never A Question of Being Enough

I went to war with myself because of you.
Not just you
But you, you, and you as well
A collective you
To everyone who asked me to question myself.
Treated me like I wasn't enough
When the root of us not working
Belonged to you
In the form of every insecurity that my presence brought to light
You cringed when I climbed a new mountain
You clapped for me through secrete comparisons
I though I wasn't enough
Turns out I was always too much
Turns out you thought you weren't enough
And instead of admitting this
Your ego pointed the finger at me
But this poem isn't about you
It is a huge apology to myself
Girl I blamed you
I criticized you
I painted you with their words
Not knowing it was the wrong color
I tried to mold you in their shadow
Because their image was too much
They didn't want an equal
They wanted submission
Through s partner who would always need them
But girl you don't need anybody
Tell them why
Because every single time you needed a man you went without
so you learned to go get it yourself
And honestly you're only interested in men who wants a
woman who can make things happen herself

It Was Never A Question of Being Enough (Cont.)

Good for the people who need a crutch
But you are your own entity
You bring the whole fucking table to the table
And I'm sorry for ever questioning that
Because I know who you are
I know who I am
I am Juaquiña Carter
Daughter of the most high
My name means God shall establish
And my identity is the beloved one
I will not downgrade
Or play pretend that I am less than who I am
To be gentle to anyone else's ego
I am great
That statement is not rooted in arrogance but in self
awareness
I am great
That statement is a chubby middle finger to the people who
make a joke of strong independent women
I am great
Did they not know the most successful kingdoms had women
at the head
I am great
I am a giver of life love and success.
I am determination
I am practical steps towards an impractical goal
I am something you never seen before exceeding every
expectation
I am flawed
But my flaws did not keep them away
My greatness did
And the knowledge of that
Gives me peace

It Was Never A Question of Being Enough (Cont.)

What if Beyoncé would have dated lil bow wow
When she was always meant to connect with jay z
A man so entangled in his own success
He could only connect with a woman that matched his fly
That matched his ambition
That matched his bank account
He helped Beyoncé level up
Meanwhile I'm creating internal wars over guys who want me
to remain stuck
Wow perspective is a Motherfucker because I just realized
how grossly unattractive you are
I've never seen a confidence so slow, so ugly before
That you would idolize a woman with potential she will never
reach
Baby boy
That ain't me

God: I want you to know something my daughter.
That I watch over the matters in your life. I am
aware of what's going on.

Affirmation:

I am beautiful.

I don't want to be anything other than who I am
I am a southern talking, awkward acting, fine ass brown
skinned girl.
I laugh at inappropriate jokes
My hair is nappy and I actually like it that way
My taste in fashion depends on my mood for the day
   on most days I am dressed like Gelissa from a different
world
And I know you prefer Denise or Whitley
Because their skin is lighter
And I no longer want to resent you for it
Instead I want to embrace who I am
And love that woman
Because I am special
You don't meet like me often
And while I'm humble
I know my worth
And I will no longer allow you to make me question that

Those were never flaws,
you just didn't understand my
version of beautiful.

I've learned to make peace
With the parts of me
They want me at war with
I have learned to throw away the word
Flaw
I have wiped all of my mirrors clean
I have looked inside
I have found myself
I have put down my ammo
I have painted myself with love
I have let go of the scars
I have forgiven myself

Affirmation:

I am enough.

Sometimes the most powerful revolutions are indeed, not televised.

Look at me
Loving all the parts of myself they told me to hate
Creating the biggest revolution
Within my own being
I am creating hurricanes
And tsunamis
As I rebel against critiques
Against my body
Against my personality
I know you want me to hate these parts
You want me to smooth out what you label as rough edges
I know my acceptance of them
Makes you angry
Or maybe you don't really care
Hardly even notice
That you told me to turn away from what makes me unique
Yet here I am
Catalyzing the greatest rebellion of them all
Without anyone even blinking an eye

In the beginning God created (wo)man naked and unashamed.

It's not that we fell; we forgot who we were.
And we became afraid of our own beings.

Tonight I talked to God about sex. It was our first conversation about the topic of sex. I expressed my frustration in that I feel I don't have a choice in whether I have sex or not. It ultimately lead to me asking God for beautiful sex. I want to have sex and I want it to be beautiful.

Can we just lie here together...
Naked?

Sexual Freedom (Masturbation)

My own hands
touching my own body
Sets off an alarm
As if it were an invasion
From foreign enemies
Who taught me that touch is only proper,
Only pure when it comes from a man?
Somewhere in the ancient history of the shell I live inside
Pavlov's dog became inspiration
And I only get wet
When prompted to
But something inside of me…
Tells me this is wrong
This is not natural
This is not what my vessel was created for
I try to rebel
My heart grows weak
It cannot withstand centuries of programming
But I will try again
I will practice patience
Within myself
I will give myself space to breathe and know me
Until my self, my body, feels comfortable
When or if it is ready, I will explore
Through my finger tips
The ways in which I can create pleasure
In solitary

Affirmation:

I am whole.

Oh my darling you shine just by being

juaquina she

Phoenix Rising

This space is so beautiful
It feels like I am being Birthed into the world
Again
Or perhaps for the first time

And this is my love letter to myself
Walking in my glory
Believing every syllable God utters about me
I am beautiful
There is an entire universe within me
Not everyone will see
But even if no one notices
I will continue to walk in my light
Which is nothing but a reflection
Of the son's light.

God: believe in the things you don't see, until you do see them.

Future Lover Pt. 3

Nothing is needed in this moment
Except what is already here
I do not have your presence
But right here are all of my thoughts on you
All of the emotions that blossomed
From the seeds you planted
In our time together
I have memories of moments
And I have hope
I do not know what tomorrow will bring
I cannot pull anything into this present moment
That is not already here
I can only sit with treasures
I wish I to share with you
The passions I wish to grow
And intentions I wish to see manifest
In the moments to come
God will respond by how we grow
Together or apart
Romantically or platonic
But for right now
In this present moment
These thoughts of you are enough

For the first time
I could hear my name
Being spoken
In a way that did not require my performance
I heard a sincerity
I was not familiar with

For the first time
I was offered everything I ever wanted

And

I hesitated.

I Like Slow Love

Let's take our time
I don't want to fall over emotions
Or stumble on my pain
I want to walk confidently towards you
I want to look honestly at the full scope of you
And decide to keep going
Or to walk away
It's my choice
Because this is slow love
That takes it time
It's intentional

I will not run off with infatuation
I will stand in truth
In the present moment
I will look at who you really are
Not who fills my daydreams
And if your reality measures up
With who I hope you to be
Then I will choose you
Today
And everyday for the rest of my life

Affirmation:

I am in partnership with God.

I trust my partnership with God.

Can we call him light
Can we call him love
Can we call him...God
Can we call him by his name
Can we call him YHWH

He is the "universe"

Who am I?

Loved.

What is love?

Life.

What is love?

Freedom.

To the black girls who consider suicide,

Please keep going.

One day you will hurt a little less

Then another day will come in which you don't hurt at all

But right now, the pain seems unbearable
,
Almost like it won't end

Because you have been suffering so long, you cannot
remember when it started

But if it is one thing I am certain of,

There will come a day in which you won't hurt as much

Then there will come a day when you don't hurt at all

And I pray between now and then

You take the time

To learn who you are

That knowledge will be the only thing that sustains your
pending healing

Every decision I make, you make, is based on how we perceive ourselves. If you feel unworthy, you will self sabotage the good and settle for the bad. Everything in your life will be a compromise until you become aware of who you really are. The part of you that cannot be taken away. When I decided to listen to God to discover who I am, it was as if I was born for the first time. Entering a new understanding was like entering a new world. I was able to ask for the things I really wanted and affirm within myself that I am deserving of good things. I was able to recognize and walk away from things that never served me. I was able to be free from bondage. But most importantly I was able to have open and honest conversations with God and with myself. I no longer had a desire to be prim and proper or religious. I just wanted to be my full self. And it turned out that all along, God wanted the same thing.

Epilogue

I wanted to write about identity because the past few years for me has been a long journey of unbecoming and becoming again. Deconstructing what wasn't in the original blue print and learning to build again. Learning to read the book written before I was here...when I was just a plan in God's thoughts. I have learned to go straight to the source to discover myself. Because the more I learn about the image I was made in, the more I will learn who I am reflecting. Not in the cliche, Christian, I attend church every Sunday way...no. In a real tangible way. In a 'why do I love the people who hate me' type of way. In a 'I must always grow' type of way. In a 'I must always create' type of way.

Until I learned who I was underneath the masks, I could not understand the concept of purpose. Because everything in this world is ever changing and ever evolving. Holding on to something that isn't at my core, felt like trying to grasp sand particles. Even when I thought I had a good grip, some grains slipped through my fingers. No, it wasn't until I discovered something that can never be snatched that the world began to regain its solid nature.

So, who am I?

Simple
My identity can only be found in my relation to the one who created it
Who am I?
A child of God.

So, again I will ask...

Who are you?

Also by Juaquina She

She: A Poetic Memoir

Contact Juaquina She

Juaquinashe.com